I want to thank Jesus Christ and my whole family
for allowing me to see a need for kids to learn about Saving & Investing.
I really would like to thank my parents for helping my vision come true.
Stay tuned for more Super Kennedy :)

© 2018

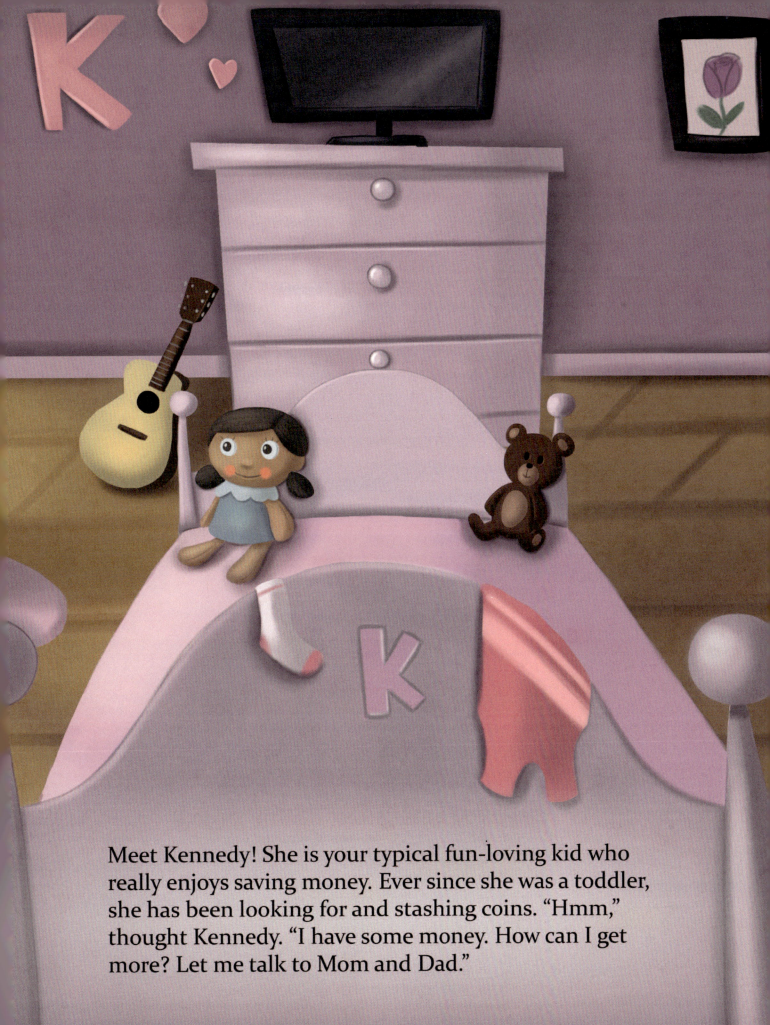

Meet Kennedy! She is your typical fun-loving kid who really enjoys saving money. Ever since she was a toddler, she has been looking for and stashing coins. "Hmm," thought Kennedy. "I have some money. How can I get more? Let me talk to Mom and Dad."

"Mom and Dad, can I have some money?" Kennedy whined. "I want more to put in my pig."

"Whoa, wait a minute, Kennedy. Have a seat and let's talk about it," replied Dad. "You are doing a great job saving your money. Now it's time to teach you how to *earn* money."

"Earn money?" cried Kennedy. "That sounds too hard for a kid."

"No, it's not," Mom responded. "You can do anything you put your mind to. Kennedy, how do you think you can earn money?"

"Maybe chores!" Kennedy said excitedly. "Let's make a list!"

Kennedy sprang into action to put her chore list together. Over the next few days, without being reminded by her parents, she did her chores such as sweeping the floor,

feeding her baby brother, Chris (which sometimes got a little messy),

and doing her very best at gymnastics practice. However, the chores did not stop there…

"You know," thought Kennedy, "I can do even more to earn money. When I get home from school I will spend extra time doing my homework.

In the morning, I will make my bed just the way my Mommy likes it with no wrinkles."

Everyday, Kennedy earned one dollar for doing a great job in school and completing her chores. Dad asked her, "What are you going to do with the dollars you earned over the next few weeks?"

Kennedy replied, "I'm going to save some, give to my friends in Africa, donate some money to my church, and even buy myself a toy! Dad, how much money can I make this whole year?"

Dad chuckled. "Well, let's see, Kennedy. If there are three hundred and sixty-five days in a year, and you make a dollar a day, how much do you have at the end of the year?"

Kennedy thought for a moment and excitedly said, "$365 a year! Wowzers!" Kennedy paused, her eyes bouncing with excitement. "How can I make *two dollars* a day?"

"One step at a time, Kennedy." Dad smiled. "Focus on doing well at school, your chores, and then we can talk about a raise. Do you know what a raise in pay is?"

"Of course I do, Dad: more money!"

Kennedy took the money from Dad and excitedly began to sing her favorite song. "I earned a dollar, I earned a dollar, I earned a dollar, yes! Yes! Yes! Yes!"

I EARNED A DOLLAR! YES! YES! YES!

Kennedy closed her eyes and danced with the buck in her hand.

"Mom, why don't kids know more about saving money?" Kennedy asked her mom.

Mom replied, "Many kids don't learn because some parents don't teach their kids about saving and investing money. I know you might not understand now, but the end goal is to buy a rental property. What that means is that we are providing a house for a family and they pay us to live in the house."

Kennedy walked to her room and began to count her money. She was thinking about her conversation with her mom about saving. "Maybe there is a way I can help other kids save money. But I'm just a kid. What can I do?"

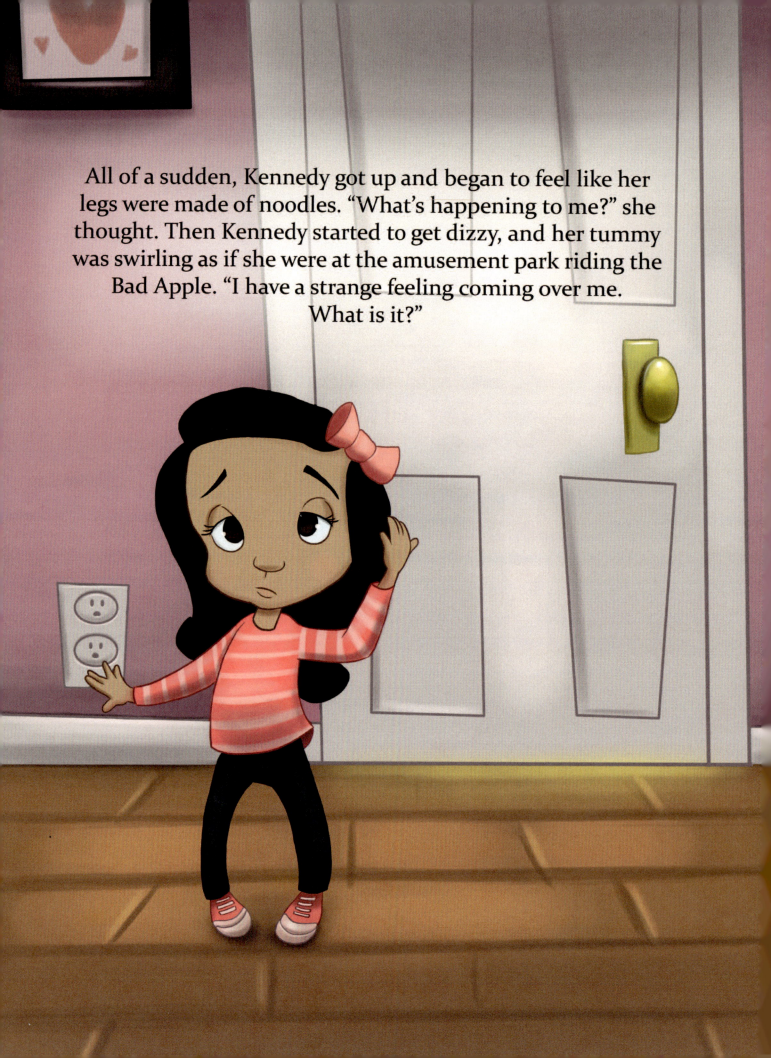

All of a sudden, Kennedy got up and began to feel like her legs were made of noodles. "What's happening to me?" she thought. Then Kennedy started to get dizzy, and her tummy was swirling as if she were at the amusement park riding the Bad Apple. "I have a strange feeling coming over me. What is it?"

In a blink of an eye, Kennedy transformed into SUPER KENNEDY! "I feel STRONG! I feel POWERFUL! My parents have taught me that I can do anything I put my mind to. I'm ready to teach my friends how to make more money."

When Kennedy arrived at school, her classmates were shocked at what they saw. Was Kennedy a real superhero? "Kennedy, is that you?" the kids asked in disbelief.

"Yes, it is I!" she responded with a huge grin on her face as the class looked on. Kennedy asked her teacher, "Mrs. Butler, may I teach the class how to save money?"

"Please go ahead, Super Kennedy," Mrs. Butler responded.

"How can we make money?" Kennedy quizzed the class.

The children raised their hands wildly with excitement. Kennedy pointed to Racheal for a response. Racheal said, "My mommy makes money by going to her job."

Kennedy said, "That's true, but how can we kids make money?"

Kennedy answered her own question. "You can make money by doing your chores, just like our parents earn money by going to work."

The entire class started chattering and getting excited about doing chores to make money.

Over the next few weeks, the kids were excited about the dollars they were making. Kennedy had accomplished her goal.

Kennedy stashed her cape away once she arrived home. She had more questions to ask her mom and dad. Kennedy had been thinking of other ways to earn money. "Mom and Dad," she asked, "how about a lemonade stand? I can make lemonade and sell it in the front yard. I will make lots of money and will teach other kids how to do it."

"Kennedy, how do you plan to let people know about your lemonade stand?" replied Dad.

"I'm not sure how," Kennedy responded.

"It's two words, Kennedy," Dad said with excitement. **"GUERRILLA MARKETING!"**

"What's guerrilla marketing?" Kennedy asked. "Is it a real gorilla, Dad? If so, can the gorilla be our pet?"

"Kennedy, you are so silly," Dad replied. "Guerrilla marketing is advertising on a low budget. This means getting the word out about your lemonade stand without spending a lot of money. We will make you some flyers to put out for promotion. That's guerrilla marketing!"

"Here are the lemonade stand flyers, Kennedy. We can put out as many flyers as possible."

Kennedy went into her room and turned into Super Kennedy. She flew off and started to put out her flyers. Kennedy's first stop was her school. Because of her super speed, she was able to post the flyers in a flash. She put flyers in the hallway and on all the lockers. Even the principal heard the news.

Kennedy flew all around her community putting out flyers.

Every inch was covered. "Dad will be so proud," she thought. "This guerrilla marketing thing is super easy."

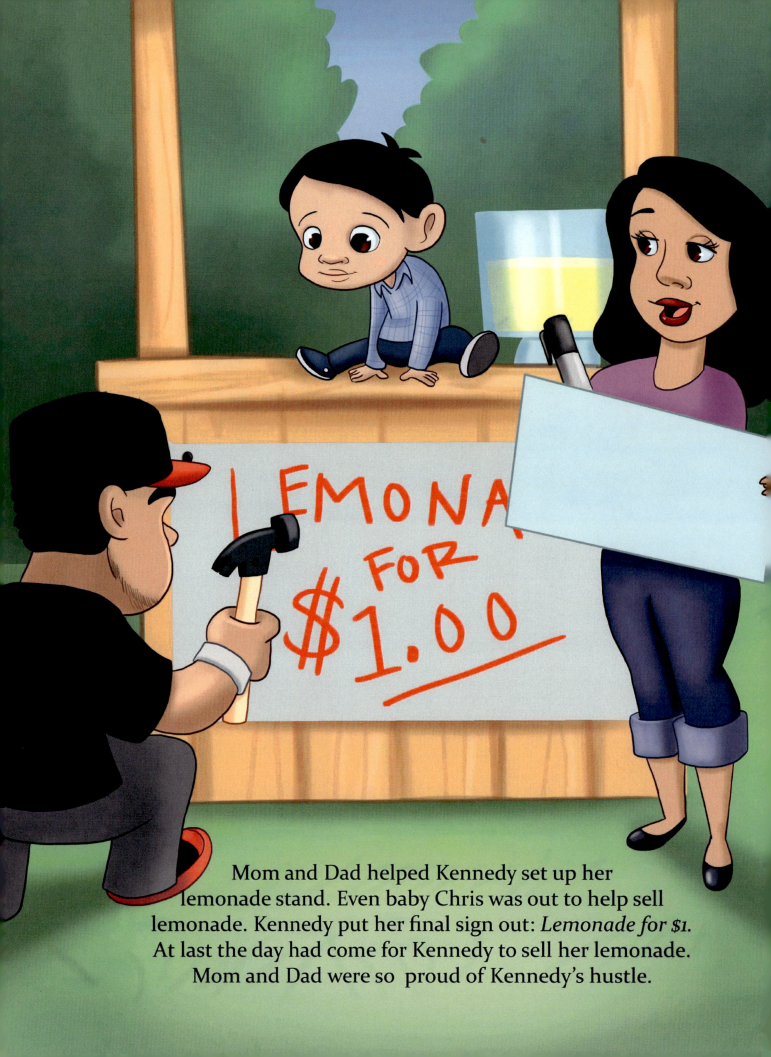

Mom and Dad helped Kennedy set up her lemonade stand. Even baby Chris was out to help sell lemonade. Kennedy put her final sign out: *Lemonade for $1*. At last the day had come for Kennedy to sell her lemonade. Mom and Dad were so proud of Kennedy's hustle.

Kennedy *slurrrped* the lemonade down. "Want some lemonade, Dad?"

Dad chuckled. "Kennedy, if we drink all the lemonade then you can't make any money." "You are right. Can I have a cookie?"

Dad replied, "I guess you deserve a treat. Now get to work and make this a **DONE DEAL!**"

Kennedy and her friends had everything set up and ready for customers. It was slow at first but by noon Kennedy had a line around the block. The lemonade stand was a success. Kennedy made $75. "WOW! This is a good example that you can make money as a kid with your parents' and friends' support."

Over the years Kennedy earned and saved lots of money. She saved money from special occasions: for example, Christmases,

birthdays, chores, profits from the lemonade stand, and money from her parents when she made good grades on her report card. Kennedy really raked in the money and was determined to save it.

BANK

Kennedy called a few of her friends to go with her to the bank to deposit her money. She not only had her cash, but she also brought her coins with her. Kennedy really enjoyed when the bank teller put her coins in a money counter.

Ching, ching, ching went the sound of the money counter. It made a lot of noise with the coins being collected by the machine. Kennedy and her friends played a guessing game to try and figure out how much money she had saved.

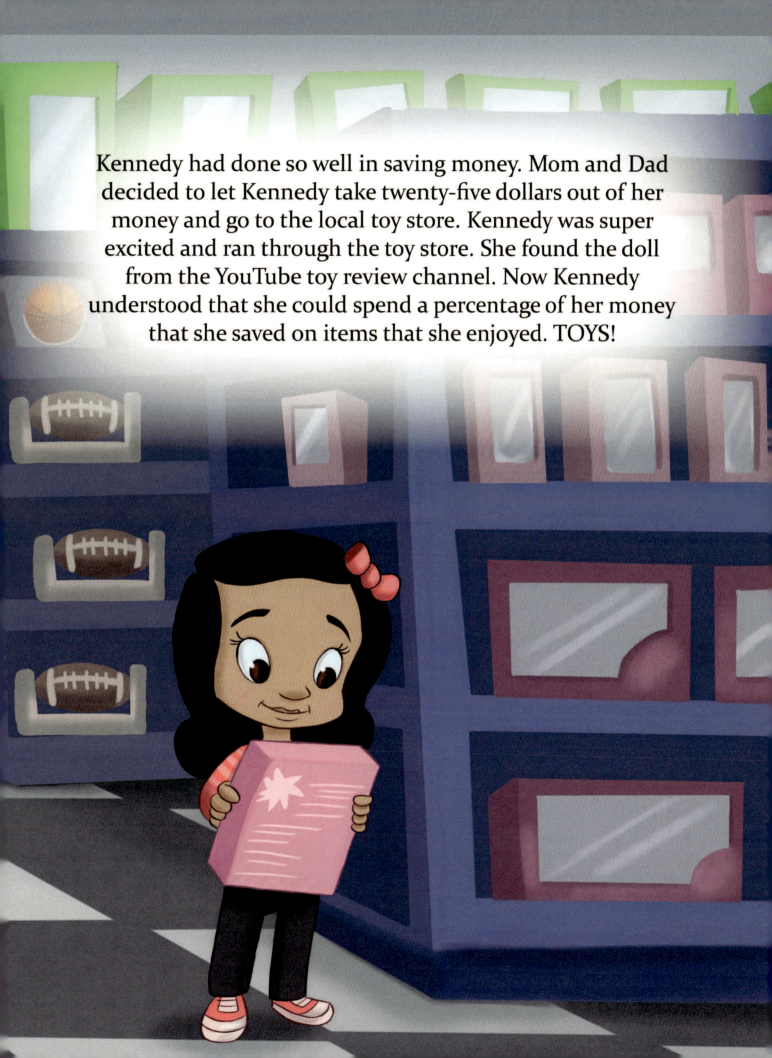

Kennedy had done so well in saving money. Mom and Dad decided to let Kennedy take twenty-five dollars out of her money and go to the local toy store. Kennedy was super excited and ran through the toy store. She found the doll from the YouTube toy review channel. Now Kennedy understood that she could spend a percentage of her money that she saved on items that she enjoyed. TOYS!

Kennedy dashed to the living room happy about her new doll. Super excited, Kennedy did a big cartwheel. She started to feel dizzy and her tummy was swirling again. "Oh no, I have felt this before. OOPS!" Kennedy turned into a superhero right in front of her parents.

Kennedy spun around to look at her family and she noticed that her family was a group of superheroes, too. Dad, Mom, her big sister, India, and baby Chris were all superheroes. "I didn't know that you were superheroes, too," said Kennedy. "Yes, we are all superheroes," Mom said. Kennedy was in shock and had no idea she had a whole family of superheroes. "Kennedy, we have a big surprise for you. We are taking you on a field trip."

"Where are we, Dad?" asked Kennedy.

"We are looking at a gold mine, your future," said Dad. "Kennedy, this is your big surprise!"

Kennedy ended up saving enough money to purchase a cheap rental property. Kennedy's mom and dad invest in real estate and were going to guide her to be successful. Mom and Dad explained to Kennedy that it was time to invest her money in a rental house.

"Mom and Dad," she asked, "how do you make money off a rental home?"

"We are going to purchase it with the money you saved. Then find someone to pay us to rent it."

"What is rent?"

"Rent is the amount of money you charge a person to live in your home."

"Hmm, how much can I make?"

"You should be able to make $800 a month."

Kennedy said loudly, "$800 a MONTH! WOW! I'm going straight to the toy store."

"If you don't have any expenses the first month, we will let you take $30 to the toy store."

"Yay," Kennedy replied.

"Kennedy," said Mom, "this house looks yucky."

Dad chuckled. "We are going to fix this old yucky house up and find someone to rent it, and make lots of money." Kennedy was excited and screamed, **"KIDS CAN BUY HOUSES, TOO."**

To be continued...

Made in the USA
Lexington, KY
03 October 2018